DARWIN'S MOON
(A Memoir of Pain and Glory in Poetry and Prose)

Tim Schaefer

Copyright © 2013 by Tim Schaefer
All Rights Reserved
ISBN: 978--0615845357

ALL CAPS PUBLISHING
P.O. Box 368, Easthampton, MA 01027
info@allcapspublishing.com

Cover art, *Darwin's Moon* by Tim Schaefer

This book is dedicated to everyone who taught me a lesson—painful, inspirational, or ironic—helping to ensure continued progress in my lifelong studies here at the University of Adversity. The learning continues.

CONTENTS

PHASE ONE: NEW MOON

SONOFABITCH (Part I)	3
TRAINS	4
ALMOST GROWN	6
IN MEMORIAM	8
NEBRASKA BACKROADS	12
SHUNNED	16

PHASE TWO: GIBBOUS MOON

COMING OF AGE	19
AND SO IT WAS (Livin' the Real American Graffiti)	21
A SHORT POEM ABOUT THE SHORT LIFE OF AN OLD HIGH SCHOOL BUDDY NAMED "CASSO."	23
POWDER KEG	24
DAYS OF RAGE	26
MEN OF THE ROAD	31
TEQUILA SUNSET	34
IN THE DEAD OF AN IOWA WINTER	39
FIRST IMPRESSIONS	41
NOT EXACTLY	43
THE THIRD TIME WE WENT TO THE SECOND-HAND STORE	48

SONOFABITCH (Part II)	49
OUT OF THE GATE	50
SPACES	52
GOT GAME	55
CARRIED AWAY	57
DAMN HIPPIES!	59
SOMETIMES I LIKE AWAKE AND CALCULATE THE ODDS	61
LANA	63
ANOTHER PAIR	65

PHASE THREE: FULL MOON

STILL WAITING	69
YOU	72
I WAS (For Allen Ginsberg)	77
AND THAT WAS THAT	78
SONOFABITCH (Part III)	81
TWINS	82
OPEN WINDOW	84
CONVENTION	87
MAN IN THE BOX	89
MEXICAN STANDOFF	91
ROOTS	93
SONOFABITCH (Part IV)	97
SEE NO EVIL	98

RANT/POEM	99
TROPOSPHERE	102
SECOND GUESS	104
DARWIN'S MOON	106
WAITING GAME (A Pantoum)	108
BLAST FROM THE PAST	110
ABOUT THE AUTHOR	114

PHASE ONE:

NEW MOON

SONOFABITCH (Part I)

I remember the first time.
It was a crisp Omaha morning in early spring
and I was four—out playing in my front yard,
when three boys came along.

They were BIG kids.
Maybe seven or eight years old.
One of them said, "Hey, ya little sonofabitch!"
Just casual like.

I asked him what it meant.

He said, "Go ask your momma, ya little sonofabitch."
I said, "Okay, wait right here and I'll go and find her."

And I did.

"NOTHING... it means NOTHING," she said.
And, "Who told you that word?"
I led her outside to meet my new friends,
But they had disappeared.

And I couldn't understand why they had gone.

TRAINS

And I can see
my mother and me
standing on the platform
as the train roars
down upon us.
She is running away.

Again.

Off to Reno
and another quickie
divorce.

Any baggage?
the station agent asked.

Just the kid.

Dragging and tagging
along
through the drama
of her broken dreams.

And so what if he misses
another couple weeks of school.
He's bright and he'll catch up.

But I did like the trains.

The cradle-rocking motion
compensating for something
likely missing at the beginning.

Clacking past desolate intersections
on night roads
where the lone motorist
waits dutifully
for the crossbar to raise
and hand him back his life.

Endless rows of corn skittering by
in a holographic illusion.

Pretty girls
of all ages
meandering through
to the dining car
grabbing hold of seat backs
for support,
fingers brushing my shoulder.
Each one a fleeting,
whirlwind
love affair.

Taking after mom.

ALMOST GROWN

My granddaddy chewed his food
so slowly that everyone at the table
fell asleep waiting for him to finish.
A lone lima bean slipped his lips
and dropped to the floor,
providing some diversion for me
when I was three.

I was good at entertaining myself,
playing both sides of the chessboard
with an uncanny insight
into the mind of my opponent,
while my uncle Viggo recited off-color
limericks into his tape recorder when
he was drunk—enriching my early vocabulary
in ways that other boys thought was cool.

Upstairs in my bed, I'd lie awake
at night, my little radio pulling in
the booming signal from Mexico.
Wolfman Jack gave me an appreciation for rhythm and blues,
and the revelation that being crazy
would be my ticket out of that lonely farmhouse.
Biding my time—

playing Chuck Berry 45s
on my lo-fi—
and anyway I'm almost grown.

A world of pain and glory looming
that even my fanciful imagination
didn't see coming.

IN MEMORIAM

Everything starts here
in my composition book
just like the ones I never used
for school work
too busy scribbling my subversive poetry
in study hall
a nasty little parody of *Beowulf*
or *The Night Before Christmas*
a drunken Santa staggering around
busting up the furniture
always thought drunks were funny
still do
art imitating life
I guess
I was past the days when dad
barely able to stand
took the car out one New Year's Eve
and wrecked it
injuring some innocent family members
in the other vehicle
then
somehow getting a ride back home
and taking our other car out
and wrecking it the same night

the guy was a gas

one day I said this is such B.S.
the idea of school as a full time job
and I vowed to stop taking homework
completely
and made good on it
my last two years of high school
nobody cared
the funniest thing was
they let me graduate
dear old Mom and her Second Big Mistake
would be at the beer joints all night
I'd stay up alone on Saturdays
in that isolated farmhouse
watching Boris Karloff and Bela Lugosi
on late night TV
I wanted to walk like an Egyptian
I could always count on them
to come home fighting
ripping the phone out of the wall
and busting up some furniture
so comical
I'd pass my nasty rhymes around in class
Teach would be up there with his blah blah
my poem circulating up and down
each row of desks
even the girls snickering
and passing it on
and Teach

protector of impressionable minds
intercepting the paper
beginning to read
beginning to laugh out loud
catching himself
face turning red
going on a diatribe about how such trash
was the product of a sick mind
but it was too late
be had already tipped his hand
and good ol' Mom lying there
in a pile of chicken feathers
from a ripped up pillow
and ol' Doc from town would come out
and patch her up
discreetly
it was a small town
and Doc's young daughter
prettiest girl in my junior high class
asked me out one time
went to a roller skating party
it occurred to me much later
that he must have put the kibosh
on that from ever happening again
with the likes of me
and Santa cursed
and flipped them all the bird

as he rode out of sight
after busting up some furniture of course
always thought drunks were funny
still do
but only if they are funny
and not morose
more points if he's staggering around
with a lampshade on his head
every comic knows
that comedy comes from pain
so please don't stand there
with that look of disdain
and try to change me now

NEBRASKA BACKROADS

So I was watching this news show about teenagers and how stupidly mean and cruel they can be to one another, and that more recent phenomenon: online bullying. Suddenly, I flashed back to Eileen. Hadn't thought about her for eons. On a whim, I decided to look her up online. I've had little success trying to find people with ordinary surnames. It's the proverbial needle in the haystack you'll never find unless it pokes you in the butt. But Eileen's last name was unique. I figured there couldn't be more than one of her floating around out there, and I was right. I typed in her full name and hit enter.

And there it was. A whole extended family photo album from back in the day, right up to nearly present time, had been transferred to the net, with identifying captions.

I began to scroll.

We were both 14, eighth graders in that tiny town. She was sort of cute, and I was attracted to her. One day I found myself walking her home. Somewhere along the way we stopped and engaged in a long, sweet, warm embrace. An innocent but romantically charged kind of thing, to be sure.

Then one night a bunch of us kids were out joyriding, and I ended up in the rear seat of the car as it wended its way along a dark Nebraska backroad. Eileen was sandwiched in between me and one of our classmates—I'll call him "Buzz." I was thinking this might be another opportunity for me and Eileen to get cozy.

And then—

I looked over and Buzz was making out with her. And he was feeling her up.

Everywhere.

And she was letting him. A myriad of emotions swirled around in my head. I was a bit behind on the learning curve, but it didn't take long to catch up. Eileen was the first "loose" girl I'd ever encountered close up.

After a few minutes there was a break in the action, and Buzz looked over at me and said, "Take over!"

Eileen looked at me expectantly. Now, had we all been ten years older, my response might have drawn some raised eyebrows, and likely some comments about me being a kinky sort of cat. But none of us were even close to being that sophisticated at the time. And the fact is, I was nervous. And my sense of it was, at that point, she was already damaged goods. So I said, "That's okay. I'd rather just watch."

A couple days later the phone rang. Eileen was on the line. Before I could get a word out, she called me a few choice names. Then she said she was calling to tell me that nobody liked me. In fact, everybody hated me. I was taken aback. Where was all this coming from? I couldn't believe that a girl I was in the clinches with just a few days earlier could turn so hateful and mean. And I will always believe that she started a one-person campaign to turn my peers against me.

It has taken me until now to grasp that Eileen must have felt rejected by me—in her dissolute kind of way—in the back seat of the car that night. My first painful dealings with a woman scorned.

So here I am, scrolling down that online photo album. And there she is. Her high school graduation photo, taken four years after the last time I ever spoke to her. She was dolled up and decked out, and even cuter than I remembered. But if you looked closely at her eyes, they seemed kind of wistful and sad.

And there she is at her sister's wedding. Older. It's incredible to watch someone you haven't seen since adolescence age before your eyes in a few minutes. And here we are in the new millennium. We partied like it was 1999—because it was—and Eileen is a matronly, frumpy looking, rather rotund woman who didn't exactly hold her looks. It happens. I'll never criticize someone on that basis. Oh, and there's her husband. Uh-huh. Suffice it to say she stayed in that same rural area and married one of the local boys. They do look content together in that photo. They look like, well, they deserve each other.

I thought about what her life must have been like. I thought about what my life—alternately crazy, exciting, bizarre, the heights, the bottom, the travel, the glory, the faded glory, the women, the heartache—and if nothing more, the fodder for writing, had been. There's no way to compare one life to another. In the end, the love you take is equal to the love you make. I heard that in a song somewhere. But I will admit to what I felt for a small moment when I had finished looking at that photo album.

It was a feeling of triumph.

SHUNNED

Worthless.
You'll never amount to anything.
You're not like us.
We've always done what we were told.
Always done what was expected of us.
Or there'd be hell to pay.
Think you can come in here
and set that kind of example?
You're out, bud.
You're shunned.
Because you're worthless.
Never amount to a sack o' shit.

But I didn't believe them.
Even for a minute.

PHASE TWO:

GIBBOUS MOON

COMING OF AGE

Her name was Connie
and I thought I might be able to
kiss her
when one summer afternoon at Jake's house
she allowed his horny poodle named Charlie
to hump her leg

With words of encouragement like
COME ON CHARLIE—YOU CAN DO IT
THAT'S A GOOOOD BOY
she urged him on
to the climactic moment of his life

When he threw in the towel
she called for one

That night in the back seat of Jake's car
I placed my mouth upon hers
awkwardly
not fitting exactly the way I figured it should
but our tongues made contact
the Eagle had landed

She must have known I'd never frenched before
but a guy's gotta start somewhere
and where better than a sixteen-year-old

woman of the world
who had kissed a lot of guys
and fulfilled the fondest desire
of at least one poodle

AND SO IT WAS
(Livin' the Real American Graffiti)

Dunno what the hell happened
to ol' Duke,
the swarthiest of our little band
of outsiders,
with hair blacker than used motor oil
in that whitebread town.
Who would sit behind the girls
at the movie show
and chant just beneath his breath:
piece o' butt
piece o' butt.

Who one night when we sneaked onto the
grounds of the high school
commando-style—
Molotov cocktails in hand—
lit one and flung it,
and the flaming projectile
bounced off the brick building
(a miscalculation)
and struck him in the back
and started his brand new jacket afire,
and the rest of us cackled until we couldn't catch our
breath.

Who one night as I chauffeured us
aimlessly around town
in my cherry-red Ford that everybody recognized,
and passed the movie theater
where we saw this big ugly brute
named "Moose" loitering outside
with his finger excavating his nasal cavity—
leaned out his window and shouted
"Pick you nose, and wipe it on you suit!"
and I sensed immediately that
somehow I'd be the one to pay for that.

And so it was one night we were stopped
along a country road
chugging some beers
and who of all people came along
but Moose and company,
and he grabbed me and growled:
YOU'RE the one who yelled
PICK YOU NOSE, AND WIPE IT ON YOU SUIT!
And I marveled at his exact recall of Duke's phraseology,
knowing it would do no good
to even try to explain,
and getting shoved into that ditch
didn't really hurt, man—
no, not like conjuring up
those beautiful images does now.

A SHORT POEM ABOUT THE SHORT LIFE OF AN OLD HIGH SCHOOL BUDDY NAMED "CASSO."

He met his maker
in a Studebaker
that crashed head-on
doing ninety

It was whispered
in the halls
that all they found of him
were his balls

The crash scene
reeked of booze
and I remembered his tattoo:
Born To Lose

POWDER KEG

Ebony bodies
in the black night
swaying to the beat.

Just me and Bill,
two sets of blue eyes
in a sea of brown.
In the wrong place
at the wrong time.
We might as well wear signs
that say DYNAMITE.

Would you like to dance, white boys?
Well, you're too lovely to resist,
and Bill knows lots of these cats—
grew up around here, he did.
Nothing to worry about.

Holding her now—
but from the corner of my eye
I see the switchblade gleaming,
reflecting neon. Angry words
cut through the stolid air.
Are you talkin' to me?

The powder keg ignites—

the whole joint explodes.
Brothers fighting brothers,
some trying to get us, others shouting
"No man, leave 'em alone!"

A fist slams against my temple,
winning my attention. The agitated
dude with the blade is stalking Bill.
It's happening too fast to think.

Then, out of nowhere,
the hand of an ally—
or an angel—
grabs mine. I am pulled,
nearly dragged,
through the confusion.

I stumble into the starry night,
and hearing the sirens approach,
I am filled with a sense of dread
that Bill has gotten the worst of it.

DAYS OF RAGE

Gather round chillun, lordy lordy yes, and I'll tell you a story 'bout—well, would you believe that in these United States of America the way you look—your physical appearance and all, might be illegal? Least that's what ol' "Judge Red" (neck the color of Georgia clay) thought about it back in the day. Now, we might be getting ahead of ourselves, so let's start at the beginning.

The Beatles and the Stones had already been around for a while, but that didn't carry a lot of weight in that corn and Bible belt town. As a young dude playin' the hits on the local radio station, I adopted a similar look—it wasn't even that severe—but it was down below my ears, and that caused all kinds of sirens and fire alarms to go WOO WOO amongst the local populace, who may have been one step away from lighting their torches and getting ready to march on my abode.

Folks collect all kinds of things—and so it happened that I had collected a dozen unpaid parking tickets. That's another story in itself. But one day a friendly officer of the law shows up at my door and says you gotta come with me, son, 'cause you are what we call a "scofflaw," an' we gotta teach you a lesson!

And teach me they did. Hauled me down to the pokey, took my belt away from me (just in case I got any ideas about committing suicide over those tickets), and stuck me into a cell.

Where I rotted!

For all of half an hour. That's when my boss from the station came down and bailed me out.

Now when it came time to make an appearance before the judge, he didn't say a thing about those tickets. He just looked at me and said how dare you appear before me lookin' like *that!* You will get a 2-inch military style haircut and then come back—or it's NINETY days in the slammer for you, boy!

My head was reeling. Could this really be happening here in the land of the "free" and the home of the "brave"? That judge was a clown, but a clown with power is the scariest kind, especially when he's wielding it in some provincial town. I didn't want to lose my carefully cultivated locks—they took *time* to grow, after all. And there was a principle involved. But obtaining legal representation was not in my budget.

I told my boss about what had transpired. You know, serendipity is a wonderful thing. But there truly may be no coincidences. Turns out that ol' Judge Red and my boss—a totally cool guy—had once been in the Marines together! And the judge owed him a favor! So Stan calls the judge, and says he needs to collect on that favor.

I take the elevator up to the third floor. I am not back at the courthouse. Instead, I am paying the judge a little personal visit at his office. I push through the door and am greeted by a young secretary, who immediately begins to snicker with a fiendish kind of delight. She tells me that the judge will see me shortly, but first, he would like me to look through this magazine because he knows it is something I will be interested in. I take the mag, take a seat, and begin leafing through the pages.

Page upon page of women's hair styles.

Immediately, I know what the game is going to be. And that quickly, I have determined my strategy. The ol' judge is trying to humiliate me. But I find it humorous. And pathetic. When you've been subjected to the townsfolk slowing their cars when they see you walking down the street, and their kids are literally hanging out the windows, laughing and pointing fingers at you (DUDE LOOK LIKE A LADY), something as lame as this isn't going to unnerve me.

The judge will see you now. I go in and sit down, facing

him across the expanse of his big desk. He asks me if I found the magazine to be useful. I say something innocuous like, oh sure, with an unruffled smile on my face.

But the judge is not smiling.

His face is turning crimson. He asks me why I wear my hair the way I do. I could have gone on a jag about how this is America, freedom of expression, and why should anybody care? But I don't. I am feeling compassionate toward him, at least to the point where I don't want to trigger some massive heart attack.

I tell him that I am in the entertainment business, and it's all part of my "image." He scoffs. And then something strange. Judge Red is shaking. His hands. His whole body. Trembling. With *rage*. He is torn between what he knows he would like to do to me, and keeping his word to his old military buddy.

I had never in my life seen that level of hatred directed toward me from someone who didn't know me in the slightest, or what I was about, or anything I stood for. But surely, if I had the audacity to wear my hair an inch or two below my ears, I must be some kind of *dangerous, radical, subversive, pinko, anarchist, commie spy!*

It was a different time.

I had played it perfectly, though. (If you can keep your head when all those about you are losing theirs...) He said that it would be a ten dollar fine on the parking tickets. Now get the hell outta my office.

The ten bucks was less than what I would have paid to settle *one* of those twelve tickets had I "done the right thing" and paid them on time.

The wheels of justice turn in mysterious ways.

MEN OF THE ROAD

Rub-a-dub-dub
three guys in a club
called Boys Town
just across the Mexican line
and I was lookin' so fine

When she came over to me
so fresh-faced
in what must have been
a blonde wig

I tried to read
her body language
but it was in Spanish
and the only words I knew
were *quanto es?*

And

While ultimately
legal tender
was exchanged
for counterfeit love
there was something there
that fit like a glove
and she wanted me to spend

the night
with the meter turned off

But

We were men of the road
and it was time to hit it
Just outside of town
we spotted a peasant
lying prone in the ditch
drunk
or maybe dead

Jake stopped the car
and went sprinting back there
(thought maybe he was concerned)
but he came trotting back
with the man's straw hat in hand
and he wore that trophy
all the way to Panama
Our code of the road
had been set
though we were still wet
behind the ears
we roared on outta there
lookin' for adventure
in whatever came our way

Still eons away
from the day
when the Sweet Bird Of Youth
would take a massive crap
on our windshield

TEQUILA SUNSET

Their gracious host
The Good Samaritan Veterinarian
grabs the gringa
and bolts for the door of the cantina

A mad dash
and a merry chase
across a Mexico City park ensues

Farm Boy
who has only an hour's familiarity
with the healing properties of tequila
sensing that shortly
it will purge his system
is now playing catch up

Should have seen it coming
down here
with her blonde hair
blue eyes
and white Levis

Back at the "Pukemobile"
(it ain't easy bein' green)
all are polite
in the gilded night

The doc generously offers to drive
in fits and starts
down dead-end streets
back tracking
plowing over road signs
and in the back
laying low
Farm Boy narrowly avoids
the blow back of his paramour's barf
out the open window
into the warm breeze
of a tropical night
(the old Beetle living up to its handle at last)

At the hotel
two boys on the steps
look quizzically at the little entourage
as Boy volunteers *"Borracho"*
by way of explanation
They shake their heads knowingly
already familiar
in their tender years
with the spectacle
of shit-faced gringos
bouncing off the walls
with lecherous Latinos
in hot pursuit

Regrouped sufficiently now
to wonder
can they reach the room in time
to ditch the doc
but his foot wedged
inside the door
brings the promise of more

Boy hangs on desperately
to the bed
as the room spins
like a carnival ride

You are sick my friends
Samaritan says
(another debt of gratitude they owe—
the animal doctor has diagnosed them for free!)
providing wet towels
for their heads

There is a lull in the action…

Then…

Squirming
kicking
biting

cussing
and disparaging his ancestry
Blondie's jeans
are down
around
her ankles
the bespectacled
man of medicine
lowering himself onto her...

But access to the moving target
is denied
a momentary stalemate
as in the spaghetti westerns
right before the *climactic* scene...

(Boy's passivity stems not only
from an inability to discern up from down
but out of a morbid curiosity
to see how she will handle it—
having invited the "nice man" for a drink
against his better judgment)

The question becomes moot
as the doc
feeling he's beat
appears to be heading for the door

but not before
he takes matters into his own hand
and stops to fire a parting shot
across the bow
his aim true
strafing the both of them with his seed
as they lie there
too pathetic
and stupefied
to care

IN THE DEAD OF AN IOWA WINTER

It was a brilliant scheme. Five guys and me, calling the same house home. Thirty-five bucks apiece and that paid for a month's rent. It worked for me. I had recently been relieved of my duties at a local radio station. A couple of us had jobs, but most of my house mates were in similar straits.

Food was scarce. Sometimes we would make a run to one of the fast food joints—doing this "alms for the poor" thing—and they would donate hard-crusted burgers and sandwiches that otherwise would have ended up in their dumpster. But we had our own place, and we could drink all the booze we wanted (when there was any) and throw parties every night.

The main drawback was that you often had to stand in line at the bathroom door, as if you were on a plane flight. Sometimes there was no alternative but to pee in the sink.

I thought I was being discreet. No one in the kitchen. I turned off all the lights, unzipped, stood on my tiptoes and... the lights flashed on and there stood Johnny—the most obnoxious, out of control dude in the house. He raised his voice and said "BUSTED, MAN! CAUGHT YA RED HANDED... HEY EVERYBODY, TIMMY'S WANKIN' IT

IN THE SINK!" Despite my protestations of innocence, he carried on relentlessly. The worst part was that there were girls in the house.

One especially gray, bone-chilling day—the temperature was hovering around zero—the phone rang, and one of the guys yelled, "It's for you!"

Someone from Puerto Rico was on the line. I had seen this ad in a broadcasting magazine to the effect: *New American radio station, owned by Bob Hope, in sunny San Juan, Puerto Rico, now recruiting on-air personnel.* As a lark, I sent them my audition tape and resume. Doesn't hurt to dream, right? Now the station manager was on the phone saying that they liked my tape, and they liked the caption I had put beneath the photo I'd sent them that said, "This is not a mug shot."

The dream was coming true.

The last thing he said was that they would send me a contract in the mail. Gonna work for Bob Hope in sunny Puerto Rico. I went outside and breathed in that icicle air. And told myself not to forget this moment.

FIRST IMPRESSIONS

The target on-air date for the Bob Hope station has had a last minute setback. By six months. Some kind of red tape with the FCC. But my cohorts and I are here, and because we are under contract, we're on full salary the entire time—with nothing to do but laze around the pool during the day, and go drinking at night. Or, to make things interesting, go drinking in the daytime and hang around the pool in the evening.

When our big debut is finally imminent, the management throws a lavish bash to promote the station at the swankiest hotel on the island, the *El San Juan*. There are gigantic silhouette portraits of the deejays draping the walls of the dining area. I am reminded of the song where the man with the big cigar says, "C'mere, boy—I'm gonna make you a star!"

I'm camped out on the second floor mezzanine, surveying the party goers below. A mother in her early forties and her seventeen-year-old daughter have glommed onto me. The daughter—decked out in a white taffeta gown—is parked on my knee. I'm hoping I'll get an opening to discreetly ask her when her next birthday will be rolling around. Mom, who is quite well preserved for what I think of as old—she's about twenty years my senior—is amiable and unconcerned.

The three of us are getting sloshed, and that's not a good thing for me to do in mixed company. Or any company. I look down and see a young couple at a table directly below us. I'm nursing a gin and tonic, and decide to have a little fun. I lean over the railing and begin to dribble my drink onto the top of the man's head. He jerks around and looks up, obviously pissed. I give a little wave and duck back out of his line of vision, hoping he won't compare me with my portrait on the wall and put two and two together. Wouldn't make the best first impression. Mom and daughter are yukking it up.

A couple days hence, the "old" lady and I end up tangled together amongst the sheets. She knew exactly what she was doing, using her offspring as bait to reel me in.

Ah, the wisdom of age.

NOT EXACTLY

She's not a hooker. Not exactly. About twenty. Petite. Panamanian. With a worldly air that belies her age. Yes, she approached me on the street, but all she seems to want is a place to crash. What the hell. I've got room, and always willing to rescue a fair—or dusky—damsel in distress.

There's room, yes, but very little of it on the rollaway—the only piece of furniture in my place—loaned to me, at that, by a landlady who'd correctly pegged me as newly arrived and traveling light.

It's an attractive apartment, though, here in the "old" city—and the neighbors! I am next door to the Puerto Rican governor's mansion, La Fortaleza, and directly across the street from famed cellist Pablo Casals. I never actually see the reclusive genius, nor has the governor invited me over for tea, but it makes for good name-dropping nonetheless.

In the mornings I wake to gentle sunlight streaming through the shutters, and the tickling sensation of tiny lizards thrashing about in my hair. Tourists stroll past and comment on what they can see of my little abode from the outside.

"Governor's staff residence, most likely."

What if they knew that inside on a musty smelling rollaway sits a burping, scratching, hung-over Americano in his skivvies—smirking at the irony of it all?

Her name is Tina. She knows my name, but prefers to call me *Stupido*. I take it as a term of endearment.

She stays over. I leave for work in the mornings, and she heads off to God knows where. In the evenings, she returns. It's a tight fit, the two of us on a bed built for one. Tight but cozy.

One night she shows up with a friend. A rather rotund American chick named Rosie. The connection between the two of them is unclear. Rosie needs a place "just for the night." I say okay, but as you can see, you'll have to sleep on the floor. No problem, she says. No, I don't mind at all.

We settle in for the night. Rosie seems content, sacked out in the corner. I have no mat, or even a blanket to lend her. She's fortunate, though, in that the meat on her bones should serve as a buffer.

The floor is hard. The pavement is harder.

In the dream, I am being smothered…crushed underneath some formless, nameless weight. I wake with a start. The nightmare is real. Rosie has clambered onto the bed, sprawled across the two of us like a giant tortoise that has discovered the ideal nesting spot. What's more, she is out cold. The tiny bed strains under its burden. Somehow, I manage to slide from beneath the intruding beast and tumble to the floor.

"*Stupido,* wha's going on?"

I don't bother to explain. It's three o'clock in the morning and to say that I am annoyed would be an understatement. I grab Rosie by her shirt and literally drag her off the bed, depositing her as gently, under the circumstances, as I can back onto the floor.

In the morning, she is apologetic. "I don't know what got into me," she says.

"That's okay," I reply, beginning to feel like a heartless bastard. That is, until I consider the alternatives: Tina and Rosie in the bed… me on the floor.

Unacceptable.

Tina on the floor... me and the tortoise on the bed. *Totally* unacceptable.

"I'll be good tonight," says Rosie.

In the evening, we resume our rightful places—Tina and me on the rollaway, Rosie the obedient dog on the floor... and all's right with the world.

1 A.M. Rosie is on the bed.

I get up, grab her by the arms, and pull. She offers no resistance, nor does she move of her own volition; she is simply dead weight that needs to be transported from one location to another. I drag her off the bed and back onto the floor.

"STAY! STAY DOWN," I scold.

4 A.M. Rosie is sprawled atop the two of us again. I take hold of her legs, ready to give her the old heave-ho. But now she is desperate, clinging to the side of the bed with all her might. I tug. She tightens her grip. Finally... I win out. THUMP goes Rosie's ass as it hits the floor.

In the morning, I deliver Tina's dose of reality. Rosie has got to go.

That evening, after work, I slip the key into the slot and poke my head cautiously inside the door. A dead calm.

They are both gone. Cleared out. Not a trace of them, save for a noticeable sag in the middle of my intrepid little bed.

A couple days later, I spot Tina hanging out on the street corner. She doesn't look my way.

Yeah, I guess maybe she is a hooker.

THE THIRD TIME WE WENT TO THE SECOND-HAND STORE

She had a checkered past.
But with my thrift store
mentality, I didn't mind buying used—
(there's something very cozy
about things that are broken in)
long as it looked like
it would stand up to the
wear and tear.

One day she said to me:
Why are you with me?
I'm such a whore.

I like whores, I said.

She gave me a look of utter incredulity.

But if she had thought about it,
even a little,
she would have figured that out
the third time we went
to the second hand store.

SONOFABITCH (Part II)

The girl with the checkered past
lived with me in a hotel
overlooking the ocean in Old San Juan.

There was a little Italian place nearby
with checkered tablecloths,
where we would drink wine
and she would call me "Ducky."

The one night we were arguing in bed
and she said, "YOU SONOFABITCH!"
And she tore the ring I had given her from her finger
and threw it against the wall.

Then she disappeared.
And I couldn't understand why she had gone.

OUT OF THE GATE

It is the debut
of my new nighttime show
and the head honcho
wants me to kick it
off with "Jumpin' Jack Flash"
by The Stones
because it's number one
on the charts.
But I've got another idea.
I want to play this new
unknown song that I feel
will set the tone for my show
right out of the gate.
But nobody's ever heard
of the record or the group
he says.
But the song just works
I tell him.
And it's gonna be a hit--
a huge one.
I can feel it
and I can do my little part
right here tonight.

We argue
our points

back and forth
what the hell does he care
what I open with
'cept he wants to be in control.
But I'm gonna be the new nighttime
star, you see,
gonna put my stamp on this town,
man,
though I see the longer this goes
the better chance he has
of winning out.

But

finally he shrugs
gives in
and I hit the ground running
at seven with

BORN TO BE WI-EEE-ILLLD!!!

dnnn du du du dnnn du dnnn

BORN TO BE WI-EEE-ILLLD!!!

SPACES

Ric, Bobby, and I have been granted an informal interview session with the world's number one female singing group.

I'm knocking on their hotel room door—expecting some big flunky whose sole purpose is to run interference to be standing there. But it's Diana herself who answers. She's wearing pedal pushers and her hair is frizzed out—so much for the glamor girl image. I am struck by how thin she is. She says, "Hi, come on in."

Mary and Cindy are there, hanging out. Berry Gordy Junior's mother—a large, convivial woman—is there too. And oh yeah, a couple of crashers—two moon-eyed young lesbians—casual acquaintances of mine. Nobody seems to know how or why they are there, except that they seem to pop up with uncanny regularity wherever I go.

I sit at one end of the sofa. There is a narrow space between the couch and the overstuffed chair that's next to it. Diana squeezes through the opening and her hip grazes my shoulder as she goes by. She doesn't say excuse me. She must instinctively know that I won't mind. And while I'm certain that my "brush" with greatness was unintentional on her part, I vow that someday I will tell the world.

Bobby and Ric have the presence of mind to ask a couple of music related questions, while I sit in a daze, fondling my shoulder. Berry Gordy Junior's mom takes over the conversation, talking about her son, the architect of the Motown Sound. She tells a story about The Temptations, but the only thing that registers in my mind are the words, "Temptin' Temptations," which she repeats at intervals like a litany. The moon-eyed girls are beaming, soaking it all in and holding onto one another. Mary (who strikes me as the prettiest of the three, and really more my type) mentions something about being from Chicago. Later, sensing an opening, I approach her and say something stupid about having lived in Chicago once myself, and isn't that a coincidence! She has grasped my outstretched hand, holding onto it longer than what would be merely polite--much longer, in fact, and suddenly I'm in love.

When the party breaks up, some of us mill around in the hallway. One of the crasher chicks, noticing that she has made off with a hotel drinking glass, collars Cindy as she walks by, shoves the glass at her and says, "Hey, would you take this back to the room for me?"

Cindy stares down at the glass, and I can see the wheels of her mind turning, as if to say: *We marched on Selma, braved police dogs and fire hoses, stood up to Governor Wallace in the doorway of that schoolhouse... for THIS?*

She sets the glass in a spittoon next to the elevator and walks away.

Back home in my apartment, I fall into a blue funk for the better part of a week, thinking about Mary. Her world. My world. So close and yet so far. I am twenty-three years old, and some kind of boundary has been defined. The illusion of infinite possibility dispelled. I will never be president. And I am hopelessly infatuated with a Supreme.

GOT GAME

Living in the same hotel where you work has its advantages. My "commute" is an elevator ride up to Penthouse One, more often than not direct from the pool in shorts and sandals.

Today I check in a little early because I want to catch the receptionist, Miriam, before she leaves.

"You missed him," she says.

"Who?"

"The Big Guy."

"The Big Guy is in town?"

"Yeah, comes through with this huge entourage."

"Of course, the more famous you are, the bigger your entourage."

"He recorded some promos for you and the guys."

"Wow, the Big Guy touting me on the air. I've officially arrived."

"He was real nice." Her voice shifts into intimate mode. "He wanted me to come over to his hotel."

"Really!"

"I'm not going."

"You could get a big raise out of it, I bet."

"You A-hole," she says in her exaggerated New York accent. (Think Fran Drescher saying: *You A-hole!*)

Yes, living in the same building where you work has its advantages. For a while now, Miriam has been spending quite a few of her lunch breaks down at my apartment. Just a quick ride down in the elevator, a quickie at my place, and a quick ride back to work.

Later, when I thought about it, I was struck by the irony. I had beaten the Big Guy out for a lady's affections.

It's not always about wealth and fame. Sometimes it's just about who got game.

CARRIED AWAY

Goin' down to the *beisbol* stadium
goin to the Rascals concert
groovin' on a Sunday evening
gotta be there on time
cuz I'm
introducing the group
onstage
in all my paisley finery
and sandals

And when my name is announced
a roar goes up and
one of the hippies who is mooching
off me at my pad
said I got bigger applause
than The Rascals--
(not true, but it was close)

And I see
a sea
of adoring young faces
gazing up at me
the hero worship in their eyes
ain't no hero
but I play one on the radio

and I flash them the peace sign
and they flash it right back

Intoxicated
and carried away by the moment
I remove my sandals
and toss them
one by one
into the crowd
and they scramble for those
stinky things
and someone will probably
wear them home tonight

And here they are
ladies and gentlemen
THE RASCALS
as Good Lovin'
fills the warm night air
carried on the breeze
and even the trees
are swaying

This
is as good as it's ever gonna get
and now I'm just waiting
for someone to come along
and kiss my feet

DAMN HIPPIES!

Mrs. Pereira was her name, and she was my landlady. Such a nice lady. And I know she believed that I would be the ideal tenant, being who I was and all.

But those damn hippies.

I didn't mind letting the young guy and his pregnant wife stay overnight at my pad. I didn't mind it (so much) when they were still there the next night and one of their friends had joined them. I didn't mind it (too terribly much) when after a few days, there were at least half a dozen colorful folk camped out in the apartment, and more climbing in through the window. I didn't even mind it (so horribly much) when I would come home to find three or four of them splayed across my bed, dead to the world in a weed-induced stupor, necessitating that I would have to sleep on the floor.

But this other thing, that was taking it too far. (I have my limits, you know.)

So Mrs. Pereira is on the phone, and I knew it had to be something out of the ordinary for her to call me at work. And her hysterical tone—that was a pretty big clue too: "Mister Schaefer—the neighbors call me! The people... the people... they are running in the street with NO

CLOTHES ON. And they are coming from your apartment!"

"Whoops... uh, Mrs. Pereira, so sorry... I had no idea. I will put a stop to that. Yes, it is terrible, don't worry..."

But there was no consoling her. Like all nice people, she had her limits. And I felt bad for putting her in the position of having to tell me I would need to find another place to live.

Maybe I'm just too nice sometimes.

SOMETIMES I LIE AWAY AT NIGHT AND CALCULATE THE ODDS

She was a tourist, and I liked the tourists. The encounters were brief, but intense. With Marissa, though, it was butterfly kisses as we lay next to each other beside the pool.

She was wholesome. Like Wonder Bread. So it didn't seem right to put the total moves on her—sandwiched as I was between my own desires and a determination not to spoil something sweet and pure.

The days moved slowly by, scented with suntan lotion and lip gloss. We gave each other room to breathe, but maybe too much, for one night this leisure suit loudmouth I'd run into a couple of times stops me in the hotel lobby and says, "Hey, I see you with that blonde, Melissa, all the time. You've made it with her, haven't you? Other night I took her out to dinner and then up to my room. She really wanted it, ya know—not so hot, though, she just lays there..."

He walked away and left me dumbfounded, shaking my head. Sure, she's gonna do it with an A-hole like that and not me. Hah!

Now the days ticked off like a time bomb, and whenever

I saw her I couldn't stop thinking about what "Mr. Debonair" had said. Could it actually be true? If it were, then she was playing me for a sucker. Nice guys get butterfly kisses. Bastards get laid.

So one day at a cafe I decided to ask her point blank. But I didn't. Because if it wasn't true and I should accuse her of such abomination, that fragile thing we had between us—oh, Jesus, I couldn't. I just couldn't.

Not that it matters anymore. She went back to the states and I never saw her again. But as I look back I can see that ever since, there's been a see-saw pattern to my behavior toward the fair sex.

Nice guy. Bastard. Nice guy. Bastard.

It was the only way, you see. I had to cover all the bases. Because I didn't know. I never will know. Did she or didn't she?

Sometimes I lie awake at night and calculate the odds.

And now you and me—we dig each other. But damned if I didn't lose track of where I'm supposed to be in the sequence. So the question is, as Dirty Harry once said: ARE YOU FEELIN' LUCKY?

LANA

She shows up at the radio station one day with two suitcases, looking like a lost waif. My compadre, Dmitre, knew her and had sent her down from the states because he thought—for some odd reason—that I could arrange an abortion for her. (The surnames Roe and Wade were not in our common vernacular at the time.) I've got lots of contacts, but none in that arena, and I tell her so. She isn't showing yet, so we decide to make the best of her time there regardless.

We had come from the beach and we're meandering along the Condado when a motorcycle cop pulls up beside and informs us that she can't be on the street looking like *that*. She is in her bikini—tame by today's standards—and I had seen plenty of tourists navigating these same paths in similar attire. Then I realize he isn't referring to the bikini, but the way she is filling out the bikini. (It is June, and she is busting out all over.) Motorists could smash into one another from craning their necks and gawking, he says with a straight face. Chaos could ensue.

I remove the shirt I'm wearing over my swim trunks and give it to her to put on. The civic-minded embodiment of the law allows as how that will be acceptable, and we push on back to my place.

We make it that night, haphazardly and half-assedly, with her declaring in the middle of it, "Ya gotta understand this doesn't mean much to me because I still love David." (Right, just not enough to bear his spawn.)

In the early morn Nancy shows up, cooing at me through the slats of my bedroom window. "YOU BASTARD," she spits into my ear, and stomps off when Lana raises her curls (waking the pious Puerto Rican lady next door who had already given me dirty looks for the debauchery she *suspected* was ongoing at my abode).

I never see Nancy again, but what's a young buck trying to live in the moment to do?

Flash forward and Dmitre informs me that shortly thereafter Lana did a photo spread for one of the cheesier skin magazines. Not once, but twice. I figure she found her back alley provider, as being in the family way is rather hard to conceal in your birthday suit. Just a small bump, you might say, on her road to sleazy stardom. I think about trying to locate some back issues to see if I can find her. But then I say why bother.

Been there. Done that.

ANOTHER PAIR

I don't know how she knew. But I had my suspicions. I'd just gotten off the plane from San Juan, took my taxi ride to the hotel, and had just finished checking in.

I turned, and there she was.

She knew me. Well, knew my name anyway. My radio name. But how could that be? No one in all of south Florida knew I was flying in that night. Or when I would arrive. Or where I'd be staying. Except the PD at the station where I would be starting my new gig. Was he trying to do me a favor?

She was the unofficial welcome wagon--aka radio "groupie." Radio groupies differ from rock groupies only in the sense that rock groupies hang out at a live performance and try to worm their way backstage; radio groupies show up at the back door and try to worm their way into the studio.

Or they call the direct contest line into the control room.

"Hi, whatcha doin?"

"Playing music and talking on the radio."

"That's cute." (Breathy voice.) "You wanna guess what I'm doing right now?"

It was flattering, in a way, that this one had gotten wind of the new "jock" and had taken it upon herself to beat everyone else to the punch. We chatted for a while, and I could see it in her eyes. She was expecting me to invite her up to my room. But I was tuckered, and I excused myself as politely as I could. And frankly, she wasn't my type.

Not that I was like those square-jawed guys in the movies who, for some reason, always declined when some absolutely gorgeous woman comes onto them in a moment of weakness. (Those dudes had a sexual identity problem!) Sure, I would find myself doing the same—occasionally—but when you have a drawer that's already crammed full of socks, there's no reason to try to stuff another "pair" inside there.

PHASE THREE:

FULL MOON

STILL WAITING

Been sittin round drinkin
and just got to to thinkin
bout what I got and what I ain't
and why I don't just go home
but sure as I do I'll miss it
cause I'm still waiting for The Revolution.

Now I ain't got fifteen hippies
sleepin on my floor,
and a couple others tryin to crawl in
through the window,
and some chick I never seen before
in my shower when I get up to take a leak—
all laughin and pokin fun at me
for havin a job I go to in the mornings.

And I ain't got no sweet young thing
that I call my old lady,
but I got an old lady
that I call my old lady,
and I ain't got hair
down to my ass,
but I got some on it.
And I'm still waiting for The Revolution.

Ain't got two fingers to flash y'all the peace sign,

but I got one in the middle
that seems to work better these days,
and I ain't feedin my head
or listenin to The Dead,
but I'm livin the high life just the same
thanks to Mr. Miller.
Still waiting for The Revolution.

And there's no Tricky Dick
to sell me a used car,
or that phony war to tug at my gut--
there was only Slick Willie
who didn't inhale
still pullin our leg.
Still waiting for The Revolution.

No Gil Scott-Heron spittin angry words
goin round and round on my turntable
the closest to you-know-what he ever got,
and my giant Stokely Carmichael poster
is off the wall,
but aren't we all,
and I ain't got no Jimi or Janis
or Ten Years After,
but now it's more than FORTY years after
and here I sit.
Still waiting for The Revolution

Now I know I had my mojo workin
at one time or another
but I think the batteries went dead,
and it's probably just as well
cause nobody wants to make it anymore
at the drop of a hat,
but lots of folks are willin to pass theirs around
if I'll just put somethin in it.
Still waiting for The Revolution.

And maybe I did lose a few billion
brain cells somewhere along the way,
and maybe my personality's a little wooden,
but I'm no dummy,
cause there's somethin in those youthful eyes
I think I recognize—
you with the dreadlocks
and your little friend with the nipples
grandstanding beneath her shirt.
Yeah
it's that look that's more hopeful than wise,
cause I can see that you
are waiting for The Revolution too.

YOU

I first saw you pouting
in the magazine I hid in my bedroom
when I was twelve—
the year I resolved that breasts
were the coolest thing since Elvis Presley.
I was looking for the secret in your eyes
but they never revealed it...
and I still don't know who you are.

I was eighteen,
a bit of a late bloomer,
you already a faded rose
when you gave me that first driving lesson
in the front seat of my Chevy—
and though you'd been around the block
you failed to warn me that a steering wheel
lodged in one's butt crack on a deserted
Missouri backroad
makes for an unsteady ride.

Seventeen summers were yours
and I'd chalked up twenty-two
on the night of our first cautious caress—
all the perfumed blossoms and you
sending me into sensory overload.
I was getting good in the clinches

and there in your backyard you pleaded with me
to climb through your bedroom window
and go for the gusto
play it fast and loose while your parents—
too square to have a clue—
were zonked out down the hall.

Discretion proved the better part of valor
until the night at Fat Bruce's house
where we made up for lost time—
sleepless in Cedar Rapids—
while he scoured the city for belladonna
or nutmeg
or anything that might give him some altitude.

You left me high and dry in Key West
when you hit the road with my friend,
and I still don't know who you are.

I met you again in the summer
in Panama
where you told me I must have had some upbringing
because I held my fork continental style,
not realizing I was left-handed
and it just seemed a more natural way to maneuver.
Back at the hotel we put the moves on each other—
every afternoon the rains came,

and we followed suit.
I screwed
my companions
and we headed north in your green Beetle.

When we had used up all of Latin America
you dumped me at the Newport Beach bus station
with fifty bucks left in my pocket,
trying to explain how you didn't like goodbyes.
And I still don't know who you are.

Once I stole you away from my buddy
who had spent one night with you
and showed up at your room the next morning
to find us tangled among the sheets.
You said you'd once worked as a courier
for certain underworld concerns,
and the aura of intrigue
clung to you like cobweb.

Trying to clear customs
from a three-day sojourn to Curacao,
we were invited into the back room
for an intimate inspection of our belongings.
And I still don't know who you are.

One winter you took the elevator
up to the station in Penthouse One.
I slapped on the long version of
"In--A-Gadda-Da-Vida"
and stood monitoring its progress
through the plate glass window
as you got into the groove
and did what you said you'd do over the phone—
on your knees there on the roof garden
the lights of San Juan shimmering around us.

When your girlfriend came outside
I flinched.
You didn't miss a beat.
And I still don't know who you are.

I've seen you on the streets of
L.A., New York, London, and Paris—
brushing by me as you head
in the opposite direction
and I study your face for the answer.

You've dogged my tracks
and I've hounded your trail
through so many lifetimes
I've lost count

and still you return—
to a poetry gathering
where you try to be inconspicuous
but I know that you're here

for when I glanced around the room
our eyes locked for just a moment...
then you looked away.

YOU know who you are.

I WAS
(for Allen Ginsberg)

I was half awake when I
heard that the poet was dead.
Thirty seconds devoted to the man
in the middle
of the ten o'clock news.
I was searching for a line,
trying to find the missing link

between

stanzas. I was looking for
a sense of completion as he
completed his sentence
and closed the book.

I was wondering how many
others would pick up their pens
to scribble hasty tributes
before killing the light.

I was searching for my own words,
but borrowed some of his:
There, rest. No more suffering
for you. I know where you've
gone, it's good.

AND THAT WAS THAT

Whatever happened to hot apple pies
cooling on the window sill,
Norman Rockwell calendars,
and long romantic walks in the park?

And whatever happened to Ozzie and Harriet,
holding hands,
and hula hoops?

Whatever happened to cuddling
on the back porch swing,
men wearing hats,
and
women without bras?

Whatever happened to pulp fiction,
poodle skirts and Parcheesi,
slow dancing,
the strong silent type,
and
women without bras?

Whatever happened to family picnics,
bouncing the kids upon our knee,
Sundays at grandma's house,
draft card burning,

civil disobedience,
bad acid trips,
wife swapping,
women without bras,
and horizons without limits?

It was a summer's day in 1986—
I remember it well.
I was strolling through the mall,
and being the observant fellow that I am,
I noticed that all the bosoms were unbound,
unfettered,
free to be all they could be--
to jig and joggle,
to wobble and weave,
to bob and bobble,
to bank and roll
with the normal ups and downs
of everyday existence.

Then,
the very next day,
as if by some cosmic signal from
THE GREAT GOOGLY-MOOGLY

all
the

women
put
their
bras
back
on

And that was that.

And a colder wind has blown o'er the land,
but sometimes I still long for the good ol' days
when the nips that nourished a nation
were proudly displayed
through the milk of human kindness
and in the interest of full disclosure--
no fakes, forgeries, or false impressions given.

And I guess I should just forget about the past--
make a clean breast of it,
and end this uplifting tale.

But sometimes I can't help but wonder.

Whatever happened to hot apple pies
cooling on the window sill
long romantic walks in the park
and...

SONOFABITCH (Part III)

One day Dmitre, my best old childhood buddy
came to see me in Tucson.
I met him at the airport and we hugged
and he said, "You ol' sonofabitch!"
We caught up on things and downed a few,
then we downed a couple more.

Before you knew it, the days had flown by
and I was taking him back to the airport,
where he did this funny bit,
singing "We'll meet again
don't know where
don't know when."

And then he disappeared.

Two weeks later a phone call--
he'd been in a bad car wreck
en route to his new job in D.C.,
and was lying in a coma in a Texas hospital.
Two days after that, he departed this world
without regaining consciousness.

And I couldn't understand why he had gone.

TWINS

The program director thought of me
as antisocial
seems like you'd prefer to work alone
is how he put it
so he puts me on the graveyard shift
just me and the tunes
spinning deep into the night
on the AM side--
but oh, over on the FM
separated by a plate glass window
was this little sweet-faced gal
who kept that side of things hummin'
we kept each other awake
through the long hours
I'd be on the phone
playing counselor to some
crazed insomniac listener
and she'd be there in front
of that window making faces
and hand gestures to try to
distract me
we were so bored
but then one night she pulled
up her shirt
and pressed her identical twins
flush against that glass

and I was off that phone
in a New York nanosecond
don't know what the hell
that boss was thinkin'
putting the two of us
in close proximity
with nothing but time
and each other
on our hands
but I owe it all to
my misanthropic personality

OPEN WINDOW

the cars
rumble past
and from their
open windows
you hear cackling
or cussing
or some kind of rap crap
an angry young man
shoutin' bout
bitches and hos
with his finger up his nose
I'm tired of hearing
the angry young man
through your open window
don't care if he's black
or white
I've been that guy
the rallies
and the marches
righteous indignation
like you wouldn't believe
students commandeering
the dean's office
and getting dragged
out by their heels
do you know

how that feels?
there was Haldeman
Erlichman
and Dean
and student bodies
lying dead
on the campus green
hey
at least we stood
for something
besides gangsta worship
all the angry young men
who don't know
what they're mad about
every generation sees
them come and go
you don't live
in the ghetto
and the only thing
you have
to complain about
is your pants
are falling down
cuz they're too baggy
and I'm tired
of hearing the
angry young man

railing
through your open window
you think you've got
something to prove
but in truth
you've got nothing to lose
but your youth
so convinced
that you'll always be
the malcontent
but I'll tell you what
it all comes to naught
and a house
in the suburbs
in the end

CONVENTION

They came from California, and Texas, and Philly—with ideas that were all over the map. The critically acclaimed and the self-acclaimed, gathered together for three days of readin', writin', and regurgitatin'.

A hundred intrepid writers... and me... there of a morbid curiosity, determined not to listen to anything with too much conviction, lest I turn stupid again and self-conscious about my work.

A haven where, for a fee, the voiceless can have their manuscripts—and womanlyscripts—poked, prodded, and given a thorough physical by an expert word surgeon who then conducts an emergency operation—first to remove the guts, then to take out the heart, then to hand it back to you and say, "You can sew it up now!" (A woman beside me is quietly sobbing over her treatise... which didn't pull through the operation.)

In a workshop exercise, an author tells us to write a story—in ten minutes' time—based on the fable of Cain and Abel. I want to kill him for that. So instead, I write some drivel about a slob named Frankie, who walks into the G-Spot Diner—a greasy spoon saloon—plops down on his favorite stool, hails the waitress, opens his mouth to speak and—"TIME IS UP," shouts the lecturer. "Now, who wants to read their story?"

The guest poet—who is from the School of Endless Tinkering—declares that the trouble with Ginsberg was that he didn't rewrite. If the guy had thought of it, he might have taken a few whacks at Kerouac as well.

But the best counsel came from the senior sage in attendance—who, in her ageless wisdom, solemnly addressed the assemblage after the lunch break and said, "Don't go back to the cafeteria... you can't even VOMIT that stuff up!"

As I left, I recalled Bukowski's advice to aspiring writers: *Drink. Fuck. And smoke lots of cigarettes.*

And he didn't even charge for that.

MAN IN THE BOX

Rush hour finds me back on the road to nowhere—
one of the multitude of morose or comatose
wage slaves blending into the traffic flow,
merging with the stream of semi-consciousness,
farting and belching along,
darting and weaving,
to gain some positional advantage in the race to the
BIG HOUSE
where I pay homage to da MASSA,
a man whose fondest sentimental memories
are of raining bombs upon the Italians—
a place where, like a chess player who's maneuvered
himself into a corner,
they will keep me in check until quittin' time.

He appears at the stoplight
like a notice for a bill I forgot to pay,
derelict with a sign that says give me money.
I don't, though I can't think of a good reason
not to—isn't he putting in a day's work,
standing in the sun, trying his level best
to hold that placard straight,
same as the guy on the road construction crew
who pulls his thumb out of his ass
just long enough to shove a sign
in your face that says SLOW DOWN?

A man in a cardboard box
needs only to flip his lid
to observe the stars,
while I, who gave up reaching for them
when the moon hit my eye like a big pizza pie,
try to comprehend the difference
between his heaven and mine,
knowing that truth is like the sun—
not everyone sees the light at the same time.

And though I pretend not to notice him,
what I really want to do is roll my window down and say,
"HEY, let's you and me, let's hit the turnpike together—
RUN while there's still time!
Head north in the summer and south in th—"
but by then the light has changed,
and I'm back on my road to nowhere.

I guess it's just as well.
I couldn't live in the shadow of his pain,
nor ever think of a reason to be that free.

MEXICAN STANDOFF

Photo Finish! The sixth race has proved inconclusive on the replay, and a low murmur settles over the crowd amidst great speculation as to which of the two contending nags might have poked its nose ahead of the other. There are moments when one's faith in the deity may be sorely tested, for every bettor knows that if He, in fact, exists, He will do the right thing and arrange those numbers on the tote board in the desired order.

After what seems like an eternity, the numbers are posted to the sound of warhoops and dejected sighs—but one voice rises above the rest. A mournful lament that reverberates through the betting area, into the restaurant, out into the parking lot, and some of the adjacent streets as well. The plaintive cry emanates from a lanky young guy with birdlike features: "Cunt lappin' son of a fucking bitch!"

The crowd falls silent. The nearest security guard, a stockily built Hispanic woman, glares at the guy as if to say: *One more outburst like that and I'm going to have to unholster my billy-club and lay a whuppin' on this boy!*

And for a moment it's a Mexican Standoff—the guard waiting to spring into action—the guy, in his pain and anguish, considering whether to let fly with a few more epithets. Then he shrugs, buries his nose in the racing form, and walks away.

The crowd murmur rises once again, the establishment having absorbed this little incident like a sewage treatment plant absorbs another load of crap and keeps on chuggin'.

These things are to be expected, because everyone here understands—deep down inside—that a winner is just a loser still in search of himself.

ROOTS

I'm making a pilgrimage back to Nebraska, to get in touch with my roots—against mama's advice when she said: "Son, never go searchin' for your roots, 'cause all you gonna turn up is a lotta *dirt!*"

In my twenties I'd ridden buses from one end of the country to the other, and the idea of recapturing that romance of the road seemed more appealing this time than being straight-jacketed into the fuselage of a plane, at the mercy of surly flight attendants as they careen into you, spilling someone else's drink in your lap. (Hey, my crotch didn't order a whiskey sour!)

There's no alcohol allowed on the bus, and for good reason. Let's just say it's a whole different stratum of society.

And so we're off. A twenty year-old Mick Jagger look-alike sings along—loudly—to the music on his CD player. The "singing" alternates with periodic outbursts of heavy-duty profanity—for no apparent reason. The cowboy type sitting next to the dork threatens to pull him off the bus and beat the crap out of him. A woman threatens to do the same. She looks as though she could do it.

During a layover, a panhandler asks me for two or three bucks to get something to eat. Nothing unusual there, except that I recognize him from the bus we just rode in on. Eat your hearts out, fliers, you'll never experience the joy of giving that getting hit up for money by your fellow passengers can bring.

In the wee hours I shag the rear seat, which provides more leg room and a modicum of seclusion. A little kid decides he wants a piece of it too. He stretches out, nods off, and dreams of scoring the winning goal in the World Cup soccer finals—at least that's what I figure as he's kicking me in the ribs.

Later, this brother plops down beside me and exclaims, "Man, I got GAS! That's why I came back to sit with YOU." Gee, thanks for sharing.

There is no escape. And while I applaud the man for his humanitarian gesture in sparing the rest of the bus, there are certain types of misery that should never seek ANY company.

Ah, but I wouldn't trade those wonderful days of bus travel for anything—especially after the conversation with the guy who reminisced about his prison experiences.

I was getting in touch with my own past, and it was good to see the old stomping grounds again, and to meet with several long lost cousins who welcomed me with open arms, despite the fact that I was a mere pimply-faced lad when I'd skipped out on them.

There was another thing that was on my mind too. I wanted to look up this childhood acquaintance and apologize to her.

You see, one day when we were both thirteen, Judy's parents were giving me a ride home from baseball practice, and she sat next to me in the back seat of the car. Quite unexpectedly, she placed her hand on top of mine—a bold move, I thought, with two adults sitting up front. I sat there frozen, neither grasping her hand nor moving mine away. We rode like that in embarrassed silence for a good five minutes. Then she removed her hand.

Now, I wanted to tell this middle-aged married woman, with kids older than we were at the time, that it wasn't because I didn't think she was cute; and it wasn't because I didn't like her—it was because I was so painfully shy that I didn't know what to do.

Thinking back on it now and then, I would wince at the thought of allowing someone to spend a lifetime thinking she'd been spurned—and at such an impressionable age. This would be my chance to set things straight. And so I called.

Judy said that she wasn't sure she remembered me.

Root rot.

SONOFABITCH (Part IV)

Foul-mouthed little kids
on a crisp mid-western morning

Passions and tempers flaring
on a warm tropical night

A heartfelt greeting
in the southwestern sun

And one multifaceted word
connecting them all

But all that was long ago
and things are gonna be different now
'cause I don't have to take it anymore

So I've made me a new rule

If you're gonna call me a sonofabitch
you've got to promise not to leave

SEE NO EVIL

The married woman
does not want to watch the porn
on the television in our room
at the No-Tel Motel
even though we have come here
to enact a similar scene

There are mirrors on the ceiling
above the bed
but she is careful not to look up

The married woman
does not want to see
her own
reflection
at all

RANT/POEM

You can't underestimate the depth of emotion that many feel toward their favorite radio station. The station is, at various times, friend, companion, and baby sitter. And folks take it personally when something is said or done that is not to their liking, and they're not afraid to let you know.

That's why it's nothing short of a traumatic experience for the faithful when a radio station changes format. Have you ever been outraged when a station you loved—say, classic rock—signed on one morning, and out of the blue started playing country music? Or hip-hop? They've even given it a new moniker. Did you write or call them to voice your displeasure? Did you consider organizing a protest or boycott? Surely they would listen if enough people raised the roof, right?

I'll let you in on a secret. There's nothing you can do. The corporate ownership doesn't care about your emotional attachment. They care about the bottom line. Period. And if their ratings expectations aren't being met with the existing format, then change it they will. They don't care if YOU ever listen again or not. They're going after a different audience now.

Once upon a time radio stations were owned by radio people. Guys who came up through the ranks working in the business. Now they are owned by business people, many of whom have never set foot inside a real radio station before. To them, it's just another revenue source. Like the chain of restaurants they own. And the quality of radio programming—with cookie-cutter formats and glorified card readers replacing that very real sounding personality you'd grown to know and love, or, in many cases, no actual person anywhere near the controls--has suffered ever since.

She's been hijacked
this old ship of the airwaves
sold to the highest bidder
who will pander
to the lowest common denominator
bought and paid for
like the whore
she must ultimately become

Seventeen years she charted the same course
as the traffic in those channels proliferated
now she sails in a new direction
as if she were just a hull
without a heart and a soul

This foreign crew that boards
will surely make her change her tune
swaying to the beat of a different drummer
and those who rode along
for the price of a song
will be logging on with less frequency

As for me
I've no regrets
my immortality assured
in yesterday's shows
cruising the cosmos
as we speak
streaking past the dead air
of decadent stars
where someone in a remote spot
of a distant galaxy
may yet tune in one day
and laugh at one of my stupid jokes

TROPOSPHERE

Wispy clouds
morphing slowly into
some other shape—
some other beingness
right before your eyes.
Not like your life, which
does it behind your back.

The birds are doing strictly bird
things, they don't give a crap
about you and me, unless it's to splat
some on top your head

And off the top of my head
I'm rehearsing what I might say to you
tonight, if you ask about her, and why
it all turned to shit so quickly, and

I'll just say that she was the
prima donna type, and me,
just a casual guy who doesn't sweat
the small stuff--and I think it was
'cause I didn't bow down to
her, or even curtsy, somewhere
along the way. Not really knowing,
but banking that you won't be the same.

Sitting on the porch, I spot
the feral cat who lives underneath
the house, heading off on his mid-afternoon
hunting expedition. And when I think about
moving from here, I think about
where would he go in this
stark coyote land?
There's a bowl of water that I set out.
Never food.
He's lean, but he's a survivor,
and I'd never want to turn
a wild thing into something less.

And I glance up at those birds on a wire—
heads down in a heartbeat—
and off to who knows where,
'cept that it's someplace else, as

I languish here, dreaming of
Adriatic whores, and some way to
attain that kind of altitude.

SECOND GUESS

this ol' place has done
'bout all the damage
it can do to me

at long last

the ghosts of
3 dogs
4 cats
and 1 woman
are all that's gonna
skulk around here

in the quiet of the moon

one disappeared into
the desert
and one languished too long
but most I put down
when their time was at hand

'cept for the woman

who also languished too long
and then disappeared into
the desert

years gone like they
were just passin' through
nomads
on the way
to a bigger watering hole

but those sunny days
that wash over you like
the womb
create a deceptively cheery glow
bidding you to second guess
your feelings
each step of the way

and so today
I locked 'er up
and turned the key

there was a spider
restin' bold
and pretty
on the middle of the door
and I smiled
and said
go
in
peace
my brother

DARWIN'S MOON

I found her
In another century
In the remote countryside
Where none could remember
The human voices.

Given in wedlock to the sun
I told her
It was the moon
That made me a poet.

The light in her eyes
Blinked on.

We circled each other
Orbits thrown off kilter
Gravity drawing us
Too close for comfort.

Then
Two orbs colliding
That might better have kept
Their distance.

But in retrospect
(And retrograde)

Our worlds
Grew richer
For the bump.

The moon
Once closer to our planet
Now grows more distant
With time.
Yet still bright enough
To inspire poets
And take the credit
For innumerable
Summertime trysts--
But only because it's light
Is borrowed from the sun.

We live in relationship
To all things.

WAITING GAME (a pantoum)

I have led a life of great anticipation...
trading the hours of my days for the digits in a ledger—
biding my time; buying into the myth of security in numbers
and always believing that love was just around the corner.

Trading the hours of my days for that which gave me pleasure,
I languished in lobbies and watched the women of the world walk by,
assured the law of averages was in my corner—
a lonely sojourner playing the waiting game.

Watching the worldly women walk by,
I lobbied for a glance or a smile—
a lonely sojourner playing the waiting game,
still convinced that love was just around the corner.

And so, with a glance or a smile,
once in a while one would come my way—
curious, as she was, to see if love was just around the corner,
and for a while we'd fill the empty space with laughter.

Yes, now and then one would come my way,
but in the end those who wait are never waiting for each other—
mindful, as they are, of love that's just around the corner,
leaving just an empty space and the memory of laughter.

And near the end, those who wait will always hold a place for one another—
finding, as they do, a kind of purity in numbers,
trying to fill some empty space with memories and laughter...
leading lives of great anticipation.

BLAST FROM THE PAST

in the quick
roaring spin
of time
moments cascade into yesterday
like a waterfall in a dream

a flower
a stolen hour
a superpower

a viper
a sniper
a windshield wiper

spin in the eternal eddy

as the man behind the mask
harbors secrets
hidden meanings
glimpsed through patchy fog
too dangerous to share
with anyone but you

all the rocks and all the stars
the reasons poetry and symbolism exist

I'm just a visitor
a loner with a boner
in the star magnificence
an existence
devoid of meaning
and grace
the battered corpses of love
strewn along my tracks

yet still there is wonder
us
them
uncertainty
the unknown
the astounding scheme of things

hypnotized we wander

Casanova
a supernova
Martina Navratilova

a candelabra
a chupacabra
choose the next *palabra*

time sails by on the breeze

and yet
like you
I stand my ground
in for a penny
in for a pound
along for the ride
starry-eyed
and hanging on every word

this blast
from the past
brought to you by
the lingering essence of me

ABOUT THE AUTHOR

Tim Schaefer, self-proclaimed desert rat, resides in Tucson, Arizona. He spent way too many years as a rock-n-roll radio deejay—both inside and outside the continental United States—and yet somehow survived. His poetry and short stories have appeared in various literary and poetry publications, including *South Dakota Review* and *Mind In Motion*. He blogs as "Timoteo" at *Catnip*: http://catnip-timoteo.blogspot.com

www.ingramcontent.com/pod-product-compliance
Lightning Source LLC
Chambersburg PA
CBHW061331040426
42444CB00011B/2859